PowerKiDS
Readers
SEA FRIENDS

SEA OTTERS

SAM DRUMLIN

PowerKiDS
press.

New York

Published in 2013 by The Rosen Publishing Group, Inc.
29 East 21st Street, New York, NY 10010

First Edition

Editor: Amelie von Zumbusch
Book Design: Colleen Bialecki and Liz Gloor

Photo Credits: Cover Patrick Endres/Visuals Unlimited/Getty Images; p. 5 Neelsky/Shutterstock.com; p. 7 Heather A. Craig/Shutterstock.com; p. 9 Pyma/Shutterstock.com; pp. 11, 13, 17, 19 iStockphoto/Thinkstock; p. 15 Marc Moritsch/National Geographic/Getty Images; p. 21 Karen Kasmauski/National Geographic/Getty Images; p. 23 Mark Newman/Photo Researchers/Getty Images.

Library of Congress Cataloging-in-Publication Data

Drumlin, Sam.
 Sea otters / by Sam Drumlin. — 1st ed.
     p. cm. — (Powerkids readers: sea friends)
 Includes index.
 ISBN 978-1-4488-9643-1 (library binding) — ISBN 978-1-4488-9744-5 (pbk.) —
 ISBN 978-1-4488-9745-2 (6-pack)
 1. Sea otter—Juvenile literature. I. Title.
 QL737.C25D75 2013
 599.769'5—dc23

                                          2012022556

Manufactured in the United States of America

CPSIA Compliance Information: Batch #W13PK3: For Further Information contact Rosen Publishing, New York, New York at 1-800-237-9932

CONTENTS

Sea otters are smart!

They live in the Pacific Ocean.

They live near the coast.

They have thick **fur**.

It keeps out water.

Sea otters eat mostly shellfish.

They use rocks to break open shells.

They eat a lot.

A group of sea otters is a **raft**.

Babies are **pups**.

WORDS TO KNOW

fur

pup

raft

INDEX

WEBSITES

Due to the changing nature of Internet links, PowerKids Press has developed an online list of websites related to the subject of this book. This site is updated regularly. Please use this link to access the list: www.powerkidslinks.com/pkrsf/otter/